M000107424

THE JEWISH CHILDREN'S BIBLE

DEUTERONOMY

Adapted by Sheryl Prenzlau

PITSPOPANY

NEW YORK ◆ JERUSALEM

God will gather you from all corners of the Earth.

Also available in **THE JEWISH CHILDREN'S BIBLE** series:
GENESIS
EXODUS with *The Children's Haggadah*
LEVITICUS with *The Book of Esther*
NUMBERS with *The Book of Ruth*

Published by Pitspopany Press
Text copyright © 1999 by Sheryl Prenzlau
Illustrations copyright © 1999 by Zely Smekhov

All rights reserved. No part of this book may be reproduced or transmitted in any form
or by any means, electronic or mechanical, including photocopying, recording, or by any
information storage and retrieval system, without permission in writing from the publisher.

Design: Benjie Herskowitz

PITSPOPANY PRESS books may be purchased for educational or special sales by contacting:
Marketing Director, Pitspopany Press, 40 East 78th Street, Suite 16D, New York, New York 10021. Fax: 212 472-6253.

ISBN: 0-943706-35-1

Printed in Hong Kong

Contents

Continued on next page

Contents

Continued from previous page

The End דברים
Of 40 Years

The Children of Israel have been traveling in the desert for almost 40 years. A whole new generation of young people have grown up in the desert. They have heard from their parents about the Exodus from Egypt. They have eaten the manna, and many have seen the other miracles God made in the desert. Now they are ready to enter the Land of Israel.

But first, Moses reminds the Israelites why it took so long to get to the Land of Israel. Moses wants to make sure they don't repeat the mistakes their fathers made. He also wants the Children of Israel to know what will happen when they enter the Land of Israel. And, finally, Moses realizes that this will be his last chance to tell the people how they should behave themselves when they enter the Land.

Remembering The Spies

Moses begins by telling the Children of Israel what God said after they received the Torah.

"See how I have given you the Land of Israel. Come and take the Land that I swore to your forefathers, Abraham, Isaac, and Jacob. I promised them to give you the Land.

"Then you asked me to send spies into the Land," Moses continues, "so we would know how to enter the Land and which cities to attack. I liked that idea and appointed 12 men to spy out the Land."

Moses reminds them that of the 12 men, only Calev and Joshua came back with good news about the Land. But instead of listening to Calev and Joshua, everyone rebelled against God, saying, "God hates us. That's why God took us out of Egypt, to destroy us. The other spies have told us that the people in the Land are greater and taller than us. Their cities are strong and fortified. They are children of giants!"

"I told you not to be afraid," Moses recalls. "I told you God will lead the way, like a father who carries his son. Yet you refused to believe your God.

"So, God became angry and said that of the entire generation only Joshua and Calev would go into the Land. God told you to turn around and go back into the desert."

Moses recounts how the people realized they had sinned and decided to enter the Land. But it was too late. God said not to go. Yet again, the people didn't listen to God. They tried to conquer the Land and were beaten by the Amorites.

Remembering The Battles

Then the people traveled around the land of Esav and Moav, without fighting. They wandered for 38 more years, until the adult generation that had left Egypt all died.

When, at last, the Children of Israel came back to the land of the Amorites, they defeated Sihon and Og, the kings of the Amorites. The tribes of Reuven, Gad, and half the tribe of Menashe settled on the land of these kings.

But before the men of those two-and-a-half tribes could keep this land, they had to help the other tribes conquer the rest of the Land of Israel.

Moses Pleads With God ואתחנן

Moses wanted to enter the Land of Israel more than anything else in the world.

"I pleaded with God to let me go into the Land," Moses tells the people, "but God was angry with me because of you." Moses was only permitted to look at the Land, but not enter it. Joshua, Moses' helper, was going to take the people into the Land of Israel.

Moses Warns The People

"And now, people of Israel, listen to the laws I have taught you," Moses says. "Don't add to the words that I have commanded you, nor subtract from these words."

Moses reminds the people that whenever someone in the desert sinned against God, that person was punished by God. Only those who stayed close to God and listened to God's laws survived.

Moses tells them, "What other nation has such good laws as those that God has given you? So, pay attention and don't forget what you have seen in the desert. Make sure to tell your children and your children's children everything you have seen and learned."

Cities Of Safety

Then Moses set aside three Cities of Safety to the east of the Jordan River: Betzer, Ramot, and Golan. If someone killed a person by accident, he could run to one of these cities. Once inside one of these three cities, no one could take revenge and kill him.

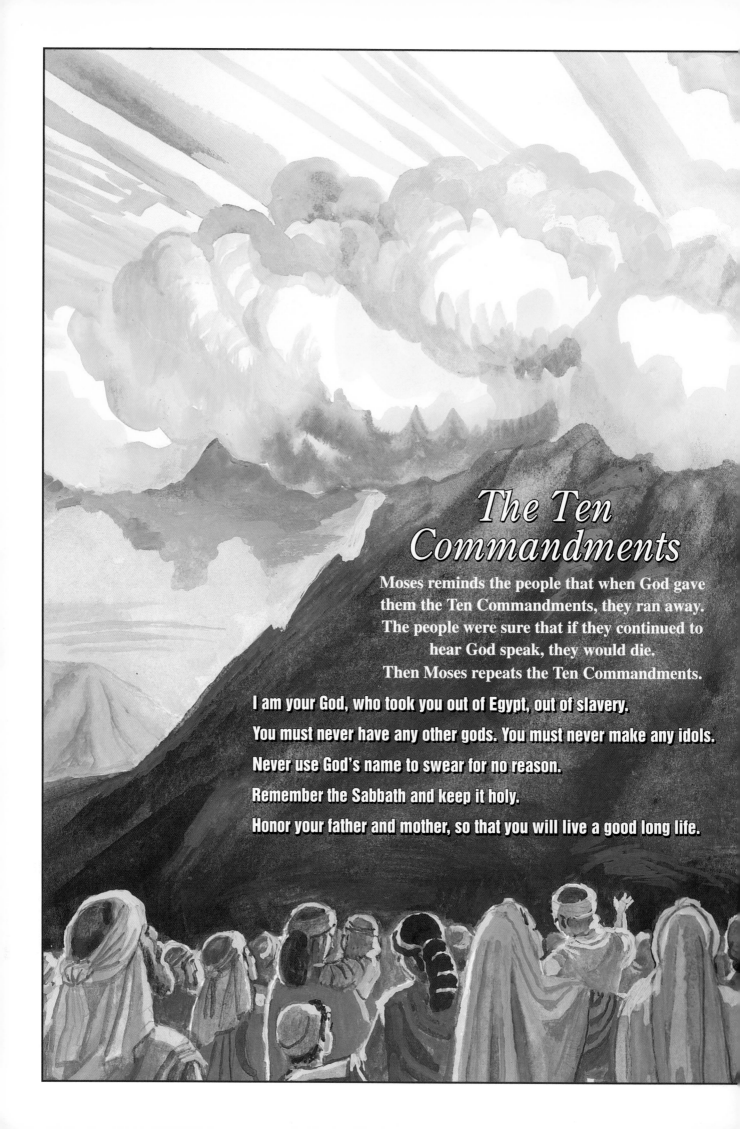

The Ten Commandments

Moses reminds the people that when God gave them the Ten Commandments, they ran away. The people were sure that if they continued to hear God speak, they would die. Then Moses repeats the Ten Commandments.

I am your God, who took you out of Egypt, out of slavery.

You must never have any other gods. You must never make any idols.

Never use God's name to swear for no reason.

Remember the Sabbath and keep it holy.

Honor your father and mother, so that you will live a good long life.

Do not murder.

Do not get involved with a woman who is married to someone else.

Do not steal.

Do not be a false witness against your friend.

Do not become jealous of what other people have.

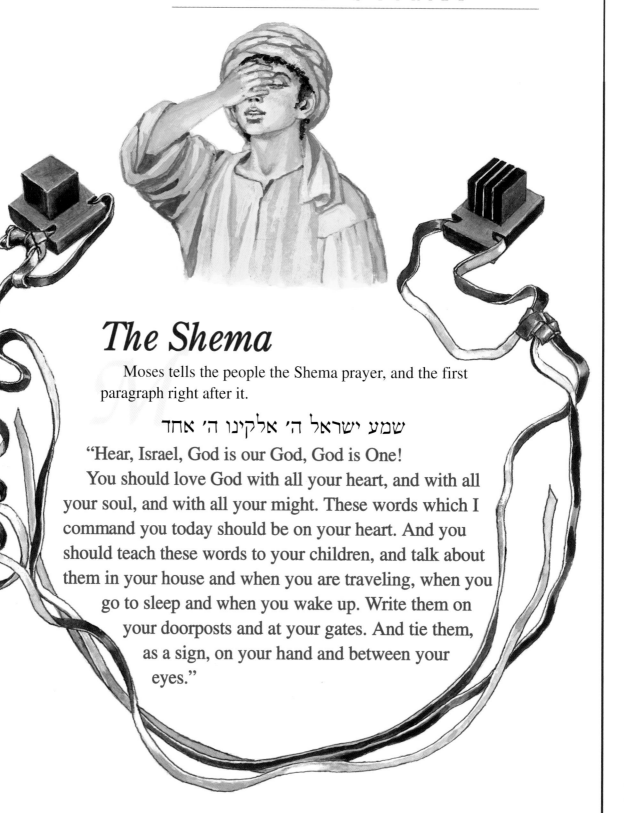

The Shema

Moses tells the people the Shema prayer, and the first paragraph right after it.

שמע ישראל ה׳ אלקינו ה׳ אחד

"Hear, Israel, God is our God, God is One!
You should love God with all your heart, and with all your soul, and with all your might. These words which I command you today should be on your heart. And you should teach these words to your children, and talk about them in your house and when you are traveling, when you go to sleep and when you wake up. Write them on your doorposts and at your gates. And tie them, as a sign, on your hand and between your eyes."

A Warning About The Future

Moses reveals to the people what may happen in the future.

He tells them that after they are in the Land of Israel for a while, they will gather rich harvests. The people may think that they accomplished everything by themselves. They may forget God. They may even begin to worship idols.

If this happens, Moses warns, God will destroy them.

So, instead of testing God, the people should follow God's commandments.

"Do what is fair and good in the eyes of God, so that it will be good for you."

If A Wise Child Asks

Moses now explains to the people what they should say if their children ask them, "What do all the laws that God gave you, mean?"

"Say to them," Moses declares, "We were slaves in Egypt, and God took us out with a mighty hand. God showed us miracles in Egypt and then brought us to the Land that was promised to our forefathers. God commanded us to obey the laws, and to be in awe of God, for our good, forever."

The Seven Nations

Moses tells the people that while the seven nations who live in the Land of Israel are very strong, the Israelites will defeat them.

But when they conquer these nations, Moses warns, "Do not intermarry with these nations. Do not give your daughter to his son, or take his daughter for your son. If you do, then your child will turn away from God and worship the gods of others."

Why The Israelites Are Chosen

Then, Moses explains why God chose the Israelites.

"You are a holy people to God," Moses tells them. "God has chosen you from among all the nations of the world. Not because you number more than other nations – *for you are fewer* – but because God loves you and will keep the promise made to your forefathers. That is why God took you out of Egypt."

God's Rewards עקב

Moses wants the people to understand that if they do God's commandments, then life will be good for them.

"God will love you, and bless you, and make you numerous," Moses says. "God will remove all sickness from you, and deliver your enemies into your hands."

But God will not remove the enemies of the Israelites at once. That would leave the Land without people. Rather, little by little, the enemies of the Children of Israel will be forced to leave. In this way, the wild animals that roam the Land will not have a chance to multiply and attack the Israelites.

Miracles In The Desert

Moses reminds the people of the miracles that God performed for them in the desert during their 40 years of wandering.

"God gave you manna so that you would know that man does not live by bread alone," Moses explains. "Your clothes never became worn while you traveled through the desert and your feet never became swollen."

God did all this so that the people would know that "Man depends on God for everything he needs."

The Wonderful Land

Moses describes the wonderful Land that God is bringing them to.

"A Land with streams, springs, and underground waters that flow from valleys and mountains. A Land of *wheat, barley, grape, fig, pomegranate, olive oil,* and *date-honey.*" It is a Land where "you will eat and you will be satisfied, and you will bless God for the good Land."

God Is The Reason For Everything

But Moses was worried that once they entered the Land of Israel, the people might forget that God is behind everything a person does.

"After God sends away your enemies," Moses tells them, "don't think that God did this because you are such wonderful people. It is because they were so bad, and God swore to Abraham, Isaac, and Jacob to give you the Land of Israel."

The Golden Calf

Now, Moses recalls one of the worst sins of the people.

"Remember, don't forget, how you rebelled against God at Horev (Mount Sinai). I went up the mountain to receive the Ten Commandments.

"I didn't eat for 40 days and nights. I received the two Tablets of stone upon which God wrote. And then God told me to go down the mountain for you had sinned.

"When I came down from the mountain with the Ten Commandments, I saw the golden calf you made. I took hold of the two Tablets and threw them down. You saw how I broke them."

At that point, God wanted to destroy the Israelites. But Moses pleaded with God saying, "God, don't destroy the people. You brought them out of Egypt. If You kill them, those in Egypt will say You couldn't bring the Israelites into the Land of Israel. Instead, You brought them into the desert to kill them because You hated Your people."

Moses also reminds everyone that even Aaron, his brother, was in trouble. Aaron had not stopped the people from sinning. Moses prayed for Aaron so that God would not be angry with him. "Then I took the calf," Moses concludes, "and ground it up into fine dust which I threw into the stream that flowed down the mountain."

Because of Moses, God gave the Israelites a second chance. Moses was told to chisel two new stone Tablets and go back up the mountain. There, God carved out the Ten Commandments again. Moses stored both the broken Tablets and the new Tablets inside the Ark.

What Does God Ask?

Moses tells the people what is expected of them. "And now, people of Israel, what does God ask of you? That you should be in awe of God, walk in God's ways, love God, and serve God with all your heart and with all your soul."

What Kind Of Land Is It?

"The Land you are going to," Moses says, "is not like the land of Egypt. It is a Land of hills and valleys which drink the water sent down from heaven. It is a Land which God cares about. God's eyes are always upon it, from the beginning of the year until the end of the year."

The Second Chapter Of The Shema

Since God takes care of the Land of Israel, Moses tells the people how to make sure that God gives them the rain when they need it. After all, if the rains come at the wrong time, they could damage the crops.

Therefore, God says:

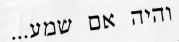

...והיה אם שמע

"...Serve God with all your heart and all your soul. Then I will give the rains at their right time. And I will give grass in your fields to feed your cattle, and you will have food and be satisfied.

"But if you don't listen, and you turn away from Me and serve other gods, then I will be angry with you and not give you rain...."

...למען ירבו ימיכם

Without rain, the people and their cattle cannot live.

To be certain the people listen, they are told to put these words in their *tefillin* and in their *mezuzot*.

A Blessing And A Curse ראה

God tells the people, through Moses, that they have two choices.

"I have put in front of you a blessing and a curse. If you listen to the commandments, you will get a blessing. But if you don't listen, and go your own way, and worship idols, then you will receive a curse."

Blood

When the people enter the Land and bring sacrifices they must remember to be careful not to eat the blood of the sacrifice.

"Be strong!" Moses warns. "Don't eat the blood! For the blood is the life of the animal, and you cannot eat the life with the meat. You must pour the blood on the ground."

False Prophets

Moses explains that the people have to do everything that the Torah tells them to. "Don't add to anything I command you, and don't leave out anything I command you," God says.

But what if, after Moses dies, a prophet comes and tells the people to do something that is against the laws of the Torah? What should they do?

"If a prophet or a dreamer of dreams does wonders and tells you to worship idols," Moses tells them, "don't believe him." Such a person is a false prophet.

"God is just testing you," Moses continues, "to see whether you love God with all your heart and soul." The people must do what the Torah says. The false prophet is to be killed.

The Laws Of Kosher Foods

Moses repeats some of the laws of kosher foods:

Every animal that has completely split hooves and chews its cud, is kosher. Chewing cud is when the animal brings up chewed food from its stomach in order to chew it into finer pieces. However, those animals, like the pig, which have only one of these two signs are not kosher.

৪০ Every fish that has fins and scales is kosher.

৪০ There are kosher and non-kosher birds.

But today, the names of the non-kosher birds mentioned in the Torah are not known. Therefore, a person may only eat the birds which are known in his community to be kosher.

৪০ Insects may not be eaten.

৪০ A kosher animal that dies naturally cannot be eaten. The carcass should be given to a non-Jew in Israel who keeps the Noahide laws, or sold to any non-Jew.

৪০ It is forbidden to cook meat with milk.

Ma'aser

Moses explains that when the Israelites come into the Land of Israel they are to set aside *ma'aser*. Ma'aser is a tenth of the fruits and vegetables grown in a field.

The ma'aser, together with the firstborn of the cattle and sheep are to be eaten in Jerusalem.

There is another ma'aser that is given to the Levites. After all, the Levite has no land to call his own.

And, every three years, everyone had to give a special ma'aser for poor people.

Shemitta

Every seven years the Land of Israel has to rest. This is called *shemitta*.

Moses tells the people that when the end of the year of shemitta arrives, a person who lent money to his friend cannot ask for it back.

But if a poor person needs money – even in the seventh year – you should lend it to him. You should not say that you don't want to lend him money because shemitta is coming and you won't get paid back. If you help him, God will "bless you in everything you do."

A Jewish Slave

A Jew who stole and could not pay back what he stole had to work for someone as a slave, until he earned enough to pay back his debt.

But whether he had earned enough money or not, after six years, the Jew who stole became a free man. His master had to give him lots of gifts when he was set free.

"You must remember," Moses reminds the people, "that you were once slaves in Egypt and that God freed you. That's why God is telling you to free the slave."

The Three Major Festivals

In the future, the Jewish people would build the Temple in Jerusalem. During the three major Jewish festivals, the Children of Israel had to bring sacrifices to the Temple:

Passover

Passover is in the spring because God took the Israelites out of Egypt in the springtime.

"For seven days," Moses explains, "you shall eat matzah (unleavened bread). It is called the bread of suffering. This is to remind you that you rushed out of Egypt." When the Israelites rushed out of Egypt, the bread they baked had no chance to rise, and remained flat.

"There can't be any leavened bread in any part of your property for seven days."

Shavuot

"Count seven weeks from (the second day of) Passover," Moses announces, "and you will then celebrate the holiday of Shavuot." Again, Moses tells the people that on this holiday they must remember they were slaves in Egypt.

Sukkot

"Keep the holiday of Sukkot, after you have gathered in your produce," Moses says. "Be happy on this holiday – you, your family, the Levite, the stranger, the orphan, and the widow in your community."

The holiday of Sukkot is to last seven days.

Judges And Policemen שפטים

Moses tells the people that when they build cities in the Land they must appoint judges and policemen. The judges must be careful not to take bribes or judge in favor of someone just because he is important.

"Justice, justice you should follow," announces Moses, "so that you will live and inherit the Land of Israel."

If the judges in the cities don't know how to decide a case, then the case should be brought to the judges in Jerusalem.

The King

Moses tells the people that when they enter the Land they will ask for a king in order to be "like all the nations." They may choose a king, but he must be a Jew.

The king must write a copy of the Torah and always have it with him. He must read this copy of the Torah and keep the commandments. In this way, he won't think he's better than everyone else.

The king has great power, but he cannot do whatever he wants.

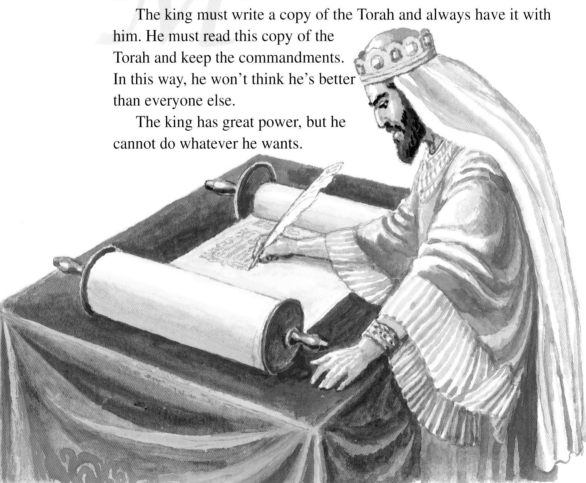

There are three things he may not do:

    ⁕ The king may not own too many horses. If he owns a lot of horses he might be tempted to send Jewish merchants back to Egypt to purchase horses. They would end up living there. God does not want Jews going back to live in Egypt.

    ⁕ The king may not marry too many wives.

    ⁕ The king may not have too much personal gold and silver.

The Kohen

The Kohen has no portion in the Land of Israel. His only food comes from the people and their sacrifices. The people are to give *terumah* to the Kohen. Terumah is the first of the crop and the flock.

The Prophet

Moses reminds the people that when they received the Torah on Mount Sinai, they became afraid and asked that Moses speak to them instead of God.

God said to Moses, "This is a good thing. From now on, I will have prophets speak for Me."

But if a prophet says that God spoke to him, he must be tested. If what he predicts will happen does not happen, then he is a false prophet and no one should listen to him.

Cities Of Safety

Moses tells the people that when they take over the Land of Israel they will have to set aside three Cities of Safety (also called Cities of Refuge). These were in addition to the three Cities of Safety that Moses had set aside. Signs would have to be set up to show the way to these cities.

If a person killed someone by accident, he would be safe in any of the Cities of Safety.

For example:

A person goes into the forest to chop wood. As he hits the wood with his axe, the axe blade falls off and kills someone. Such a person should run to the Cities of Safety.

But a person who hates another person, and waits somewhere to kill him, is not an accidental murderer. He cannot go to a City of Safety. If he goes there anyway, he must be removed from the City.

Witnesses

Moses explains that two witnesses must come forward, before a judge can declare someone guilty of a crime.

But there is a special law regarding witnesses:

Two witnesses come to court and say that they saw someone do something wrong. Then two other witnesses come and say that the first two witnesses were with them and could not have seen anything. The first pair of witnesses are considered liars. The judge will punish them with the same punishment they wanted the innocent person to get.

The Rules Of War

"When you go out to battle against your enemy," Moses says, "do not fear them, for God is with you. When you come close to the place of battle, the Kohen should tell the people, 'Don't be afraid or panic, because God is with you.'"

But there are certain people who don't have to go out to battle:

❧ Anyone who has built a new house and not yet lived in it. He will be worried that someone else may live in the house he built.

ℬ Anyone who has planted a vineyard and has not yet
   eaten from it. He will be worried that someone else
   may eat his grapes.

ℬ Anyone who has become engaged, but has not yet
   married and lived with his wife. He will be worried
   that someone else may take his fiancee away.

ℬ Anyone who is so afraid that he might
   run away during the battle.

Saving The Trees

Moses also tells the people that when they come to a city, they must first ask to make peace. If the people of the city don't want peace, then they should attack the city.

When the people attack a city, they may not destroy the fruit trees around the city. After all, people eat from the trees.

And anyway, what did the trees do that they should be destroyed?

However, trees that don't bear fruit can be cut down to help in the siege of the city.

The Calf Of Forgiveness

Moses explains what happens when a dead person is found in a field between two cities. If the murderer is not caught, then the leaders and the judges of the cities will measure to see which city is closest to the dead person. The leaders of the closer city must take a calf and kill it.

Then the leaders have to say, "Our hands did not kill this person, and we didn't even see this person. Forgive us God." They have to ask forgiveness, because they should have given the person an escort to the next city.

The War Bride   כי תצא

Moses explains the laws of a war bride. If, during a battle, an Israelite soldier meets a non-Jewish woman he wants to marry, he can take her home. Once she is in his house, the Jewish soldier must let her mourn for her family for a full month. If, after the month, the soldier still wants to marry her, she becomes his wife. If he doesn't want her, then he has to let her go. He can't sell her or make her a slave.

The Rebellious Son

Moses explains the special law of the rebellious son. This is a boy who is 13 years plus one day, who rebels against his parents.

"If he doesn't listen to what his father and mother say to him, then they should bring him to the judges of the city."

If the parents tell the judges that the boy is a drunk and a glutton, then the judges punish him. There is no doubt that he will grow up to be a robber, and even a murderer.

Lost Property

"Do not ignore the lost animal of your fellow Jew," Moses tells the people. "You must return the animal.

"If you don't know to whom the animal belongs, then bring it to your house. The animal has to be with you until your fellow Jew asks for it. Then you have to return it to him."

This is also the law for anything lost by a fellow Jew.

Being Kind

Moses discusses some laws that help people to show kindness to other living beings.

- If someone's animal falls down, you have to help him lift the animal. You can't ignore what is happening.
- If you find a bird's nest and want to take the eggs, you can take them. However, you have to shoo the mother bird away before you do so.

ॐ You must not put a muzzle on an ox that is pulling the stone that grinds the grain. You have to let the ox eat what he wants from the floor.

ॐ You must not return an escaped slave to his owner. He can live wherever he wants in the Land of Israel. You must not make fun of him just because he was a slave.

ॐ Don't treat a poor worker in a mean way. Pay him whatever you owe him right away.

ॐ When you harvest your fields, leave something for the poor.

Crime And Punishment

Moses explains that children are not punished for their father's sins, and fathers are not punished for their children's sins. Everyone gets punished for their own sins.

Shatnes And Tzitzit

Moses tells the people that they are not permitted to wear wool and linen combined together. This combination of wool and linen in clothing is called *shatnes.*

Moses also repeats the commandment to wear *tzitzit,* special twisted threads. Tzitzit should be put on any four-cornered garment that is worn.

Lashes

When the judges decide that a person should be punished by getting whipped, they can give him up to, but not including, 40 lashes. The judges must be careful that the person is not given even one more lash than he deserves.

Marriage And Divorce

Moses talks about some of the laws of marriage and divorce:

- A man does not serve in the army during his first year of marriage.
- A man cannot marry another man's wife. If she is divorced from her husband, then he can marry her.
- If a man wants to divorce his wife, he must write her a special letter of divorce and give it to her.

Yibbum And Halitza

Moses tells the people the special laws of two brothers:

- If there are two brothers and one dies without children, the living brother has to marry the dead brother's wife (called the widow). This is called *yibbum*.

The living brother marries his brother's widow so that a child will be born. This child will be called by the name of the dead brother.

If the living brother doesn't want to marry his brother's widow, then they go to the court to do *halitza*. During halitza, the widow says to the living brother that by refusing to marry her, he is doing something wrong.

Amalek

"Remember what the nation of Amalek did to you," says Moses, "when you came out of Egypt. They attacked the weak people among you. When you are settled in the Land, wipe them out. Don't forget."

The First Fruits   כי תבא

Moses now teaches the people the laws of first fruits.

"When you come into the Land," Moses says, "you should take from the first fruits of your fields, put them in baskets and go to the Temple. The Kohen will then take the basket.

"You must say the following," Moses continues. "My ancestor was a poor man of Aram who went down to live in Egypt. While there, his family grew until they became a great and mighty nation.

"The Egyptians hated us and made life difficult for us, and made us work very hard.

"We cried to God, and God heard us and saw our suffering. God took us out of Egypt with a strong hand, with signs and miracles. God brought us here to Israel and gave us this Land flowing with milk and honey. And I have brought the first fruits here to the Temple."

The Blessings And The Curses

Moses tells the people that when they cross the Jordan River they are to split up. Half are to stand on Mount Gerizim, and half on the mountain across from it, Mount Eval. The Levites are to stand in-between both mountains and announce the blessings people will receive if they listen to God, and the curses they will receive if they don't listen to God.

Who will be cursed?

Some of the sins that will bring about the curses include:

A person who secretly worships idols.

A person who doesn't treat his parents with honor.

A person who steals land from his neighbor.

A person who gives someone bad advice on purpose.

A person who cheats a stranger, an orphan, or a widow.

If the nation does not keep the commandments then they will be cursed:

- ℰ God will send plagues.
- ℰ God will send drought and famine (hunger and thirst).
- ℰ God will send their enemies to destroy them.
- ℰ God will scatter them among the people of the world, and they won't feel at home anywhere.

But if the nation does the commandments that God gives them, then God will bless them all.

Some of the blessings include:

God will make them fruitful and they will multiply.

God will bless their fields.

God will destroy their enemies.

God will bring the rains on time.

God will make sure they are successful in everything that they do.

The נצבים Agreement With God

Moses gathers all the people together, including the parents and their children, the elders, the converts, and the laborers. Then, Moses announces:

"You are all gathered today in order to enter into an agreement with God. In this agreement you will become the people of God, as was promised to your fathers, Abraham, Isaac, and Jacob.

"But this agreement is not just between God and those who are gathered today," Moses tells the people. "This agreement is with those that stand here today in front of God, and also with those who are not here today."

The Secret Things

Moses warns the people that they have to fulfill the commandments in the Torah or they will be thrown out of the Land of Israel.

But what if people sin in secret? Will everyone suffer the curses brought in the Torah? Moses tells the people that the sins that people do in secret will be judged by God. But each person must concern himself with those sins that are done in public. Everyone must carry out the words of the Torah.

Where To Find The Torah

"The commandments that I command you today," Moses explains, "are not hidden from you. They are not far from you. They are not in the heavens so that you will say, 'Who will go up to the heavens to get the commandments for us so we can hear them and do them?'

"And the commandments are not across the sea so that you will say, 'Who will cross the sea for us and get the commandments for us so we can hear them and do them?'

"Actually," Moses concludes, "what you are looking for is very close to you. You can do the commandments by using your mouth and your heart."

The Choice

Moses tells the people that they have a choice to make. If they "walk in God's ways and observe the commandments," then they will live and multiply and God will bless them.

But if they don't listen to God, then they will be lost.

"So choose life!" Moses declares. In this way the people and their children will have a wonderful future.

Joshua Becomes The Leader

וילך

Moses says, "I am 120 years old today. I can no longer lead you. And I can't go into the Land of Israel."

Moses calls Joshua and tells him, "Be strong and courageous. You will lead the people. God will go before you and not abandon you. So, don't be afraid."

The Hak'hayl Ceremony

Moses tells the people that at the end of every seven years, during Sukkot, all the people are to appear at the Temple. There, part of the Torah is to be read to all the people.

This ceremony is called *hak'hayl*. The reason for this ceremony is so that "the men, women, children, and the strangers living in Israel, will hear and learn and observe the words of the Torah. And so that those who don't know the laws will learn to have awe of God."

The Poem Of Moses האזינו

God tells Moses that he is about to die and that he should write a poem and teach it to the Children of Israel. This poem will guarantee the Jewish people that God will always be there for them, even when they sin.

The Poem Of Moses

Listen heavens, to what I say,
Earth, hear my words
I will announce the name of God,
And declare God's greatness.
God is a rock, whose work is perfect,
God is just and right, God's laws bring justice.

If you complain to God, remember:
People are foolish, not God.
God is your Father who made you,
God put you on this earth.

Remember the days gone by.
If you forget them, ask your father,
He will tell you what happened.
Ask your teachers,
They will teach you your past.

When the people don't listen to God,
God says, "I will hide My face from them."
But God always forgives the Children of Israel,
When they are truly sorry.

Moses Blesses
The Tribes

וזאת הברכה

Before his death, Moses blesses the tribes. Moses reveals what makes each tribe stand out from the others. He tells them how fortunate they are because God helps them in times of trouble.

Moses Dies

Then Moses goes up the mountain of Nevo, which is near Jericho. Moses is permitted to look at the Land of Israel, but he is not allowed to go into the Land. This is his punishment for hitting the Rock, when God told him to speak to it.

To this day, no one knows exactly where Moses is buried.

The people mourn for Moses for 30 days. Then, Joshua becomes the leader of the Jewish people.

The people know that there will never again be a prophet like Moses, who spoke to God face-to-face, and performed such wonderful miracles for everyone to see.

MIDRASHIM
TALES OF OUR SAGES

דברים

Moses gathered all of the people together in order to remind them of their previous sins. Why was it necessary to have everyone attend in person?

There are at least two answers:

- There were many people who weren't directly involved in the sins Moses mentioned. If Moses hadn't called them together with the others, they might have thought that they were truly blameless. But Moses wanted them to understand that they also had a part in these sins, because they had not spoken up against the sinners. Perhaps this might have prevented the sinners from continuing in their ways.

- If Moses had not called everyone together, some of the people who did not attend might later say, "Had I been there, I would have gotten up and answered Moses." This way Moses made sure that anyone who felt he was being unfairly rebuked would get up and say his piece.

Why did Moses choose to rebuke the people one week before his death?

- Since the people knew Moses would not enter the Land of Israel, they also realized that his rebuke of them was for their own good. He would gain nothing by making them face their sins. They understood that his rebuke came from love and they were more inclined to take his words to heart.

- Moses knew that when a person rebukes another, he runs the risk that he might commit similar sins in the future. Then, the person being rebuked may one day turn around and say, "Look, you're as bad as we are! How can you rebuke us?" But if a person waits until he is about to die, this can never happen.

ואתחנן

Moses pleaded to God: "Please, let me cross the Jordan and see the Land across the river."

Even after God told Moses that he wouldn't enter the Land, Moses continued to beg.

Why was Moses so desperate to enter the Land?

The Midrash gives the following reasons:

- The spies had given bad reports about the Land of Israel. But Moses had told them that it was a very good Land. Moses wanted to enter the Land now to show the nation that he was right, and that it was truly a Land flowing with milk and honey.

- People struggle hard to accomplish certain things in their lifetime. If something goes wrong before their job is finished, it can be very frustrating.

God told Moses to take the Children of Israel out of Egypt and bring them to the Holy Land. Moses struggled with the people for 40 years, dealing courageously with all the difficulties that arose. Now, just as he is about to lead the nation to their destination, God tells him that he will not be able to join them. Is it any wonder that Moses begs God to let him finish the job that had been given to him?

    ₭ There are many commandments that can only be kept in the land of Israel. Moses wanted a chance to be able to keep all 613 commandments.

₭₮

"Honor your father and mother, so that you will live a good long life."

Our sages emphasize this point with a true story:

There was a man named Dama Ben Netina who owned a precious gem that was needed for one of the Kohen Gadol's garments. A Jewish delegation went to offer him a fair price for his gem. Dama gladly agreed to sell the precious gem, but told them that he had to get it from the safe. After searching for the key, he realized that it was under his father's pillow. But his father was sleeping. Not wanting to wake his father up, Dama told them that he couldn't sell it to them, and that they should come back at a later time. The delegation thought that he was bargaining with them. But no matter how much they offered for the stone, Dama told them he could not sell it now. So, they left. Dama lost a lot of money because he showed respect for his father. However, the following year, God rewarded him with a rare red cow which he sold to the Rabbis for a great deal of money.

עקב

One of the meanings of the word Aykev is "the heel of a foot." The Rabbis explain that the laws being discussed are those that can be easily stepped on – considered to be unimportant. God tells the people that even the "little" commandments must be taken seriously.

The Midrash offers another explanation:

Aykev refers to the reward we receive in This World for doing God's commandments. This reward is actually small and insignificant – like the heels of our feet – when compared to the reward that awaits us in the World To Come.

₭₮

"And you will have food and be satisfied and bless God...."

From this verse, we learn that after we eat, we must recite the Grace after Meals. Also, just as we are taught to bless God after eating, we learn that we must bless God before eating, when we are hungry. By

thanking God, we are acknowledging that we realize that God is the One who provides the food for us.

In general, there are three types of blessings:

- Those said because we enjoy something, such as eating, drinking, or smelling spices.
- Those said before performing a commandment, such as sitting in the Sukkah.
- Those said in praise or thanks, to God.

ראה

Why did God make a specific law against eating blood? It is unlikely anyone would eat blood even if God hadn't prohibited it.

We can learn something important about reward, from this commandment. If God gives a reward for not eating blood, something that is easy for us to do, then just imagine the reward God gives for a commandment that is hard to fulfill!

We also learn that our reason for eating or not eating something should be based on what the Torah asks of us. A person should not refrain from eating non-kosher foods because he considers them disgusting. Rather, he should say, "Even though this food may be tasty, I won't eat it because God commanded me not to."

"Be careful to observe only those commandments which I am giving you: Do not add or take away from them."

The Midrash teaches us that we are not allowed to add new commandments or to try to be even more holy by doing something twice. For example, we are commanded to live in a Sukkah during the holiday of Sukkot. However, if someone would want to add to the holiday and stay there for another week, this would be forbidden. Our Sages compare this to a doctor who gives his patient a certain medicine and tells him what the proper dose is. If the patient follows the doctor's instructions, he will be healed. If, however, the patient decides to take twice as much, thinking he will be healed that much faster, not only won't he be helping himself, he'll be causing himself harm. The commandments are medicines for the soul, which is why we mustn't alter the dose by even a drop.

שפטים

"Justice, justice you should follow."

Why is the word "justice" repeated?

Our Sages say that a person should want true judgment in all cases. Just as he wants justice when he knows he is right, he should also want true justice during the times when he is wrong.

Another explanation is that we should be just both in our words and deeds – practice what you preach.

When waging war, the nation is warned against destroying the fruit-bearing trees in the process. It is from this commandment that our Sages learn the law of *Ba'al Tashchit*, the prohibition against wasting anything that can be used.

כי תצא

The Midrash tells us that the guidelines for defining "A rebellious son" are so specific, that it's almost impossible for such a child to exist. The Midrash says that a true rebellious son never existed and never will. The criteria is almost impossible to meet. Among the required criteria: The rebellion must occur within three months after the boy's 13th birthday. Both his parents must bring him to the court and declare he is rebellious. The rebellion must take the form of stealing a specific, very large amount of meat and wine. He must first be warned by two witnesses, and two witnesses must see him perform the rebellious actions.

The prohibition against wearing shatnes, wool and linen combined together, is in the form of a statute. No explanation is given for it in the Torah. We do it because God commanded us to.

The Midrash suggests a possible explanation. The first two brothers, Cain and Abel, each brought sacrifices to God. Cain brought a gift of linen, and Abel brought a sheep (wool). God accepted Cain's sacrifice, which made Abel jealous enough to kill his brother. God decided that these two materials – one from a sinner and one from a worthy person – should never be worn together.

It is interesting to note that the Kohen Gadol *had* to wear Shatnes in his clothing. After all, he is responsible for all Jews, sinners and non-sinners alike.

כי תבא

The Midrash summarizes the commandment of bringing the first fruits:

"Let the first (the Jewish People) bring the first (the first fruits), to the first (the Kohen who is first in service of the Temple) in the first place (the Holy Temple) to the First of all (God)."

נצבים

The word, *nitzavim,* is translated here as standing. However, usually the word *omed* is used when the Torah is talking about standing. Nitzavim connotes something more intense. It means that they stood there as a proud and dignified people, united as one.

The Midrash brings a story to explain the importance of unity.

On his deathbed, a man called all of his sons to his side. He held out a bundle of reeds to them.

"Can you break these?" he asked. One by one, each of the strong young men tried unsuccessfully to snap the bundle in two.

"Watch and I will show you how," their father told them. He separated the reeds and proceeded to snap each one in half. "Learn from my lesson, my sons," said the man. "If you stay together, you will remain strong and no one will be able to break you. But if you separate, you will easily be broken."

This is the lesson that the Jewish people must learn. When they are together as a strong, unified people, they cannot be conquered. But when they argue and fight among themselves, those who seek to destroy them will succeed in their task.

Moses tells the nation not to worry, because the Torah "is very close to you."

The Talmud teaches us that a fetus is taught the entire Torah in his mother's womb. But, before he is born, an angel comes and taps him on the mouth, causing him to forget it. That accounts for the indentation on the upper lip of every child. Moses says that the Torah "is very close to you" because it is always easier to learn something that was already learned, than to learn something for the first time.

וילך

Joshua is told that he is to lead the people. The Midrash points out that Joshua learned the lesson of leadership the hard way. After Jericho was conquered, Joshua sent out a troop of soldiers to attack the city of Ai. But instead of defeating their enemy, many of the soldiers were killed.

God explained to Joshua that this happened because he was told to "lead" the people, and instead he sent them out on their own. A leader has to stand at the head of the army if he wants to fill his army with confidence.

"I am 120 years old today."

From the additional word "today," our Sages tell us that Moses died on his birthday, the seventh of Adar.

Even today, it is considered a sign of greatness when someone dies on their birthday.

God appears to Moses and announces, "The time of your death is near."

Only two others were told of their impending death: Jacob and King David. Each of these three people was singled out as unique. Moses was the greatest of the prophets, David was the foremost king, and Jacob was the chosen of the forefathers.

האזינו

"Listen, Heavens and I will speak. Earth, hear my words."

Moses calls on the heaven and earth to listen as he speaks. Why? According to the Torah, a person can only be punished if he has been warned in front of two witnesses. Since Ha'azinu contains many warnings, Moses is calling heaven and earth to be his two witnesses. But why did he call on them? Why not call on the elders of the people?

The Midrash suggests several reasons:

- Humans eventually die. Their testimony is short-lived. But the heaven and earth will be around as long as mankind survives. They make ideal witnesses.

- Heaven and earth are extremely dependable in carrying out God's requests. The sun shines every day, and seeds that are sown grow every day, slowly yet steadily.

Therefore, the heavens and earth can serve as good examples of the way the Children of Israel should carry out their own tasks. They too should be steady, stable and enduring.

וזאת הברכה

Noah, Isaac, and Jacob all blessed their sons before they passed away. The Torah shows us that Moses was like a father to the Children of Israel. He too wanted to bless his "children" before he passed away.

Why wasn't the final resting place of Moses revealed to the people?

The Midrash says that God didn't want the nation to turn Moses' grave into a shrine. People might pray to Moses instead of to God.

THE BOOK OF JONAH

THE BOOK OF JONAH is read in the synagogue during the Afternoon Service of Yom Kippur. On Yom Kippur, the Jewish people ask God to forgive their sins. They spend an entire day, praying and fasting, hoping to be written in The Book Of Life.

Jonah was a prophet who refused to do what God commanded. When he was swallowed by the Great Fish, Jonah prayed and fasted. He realized that if a person wants to be written in The Book Of Life, he has to do God's commandments. God forgave Jonah because Jonah was sincere. So too, we hope that God will forgive everyone who sincerely wants to improve themselves.

God spoke to the prophet Jonah, the son of Amittai, who lived in Israel, saying:

"Get up and go to the great city of Ninveh. Shout at them to stop being so wicked, because I am about to destroy them!"

But, instead of going to Ninveh, Jonah got up and ran to the port of Jaffa. There, he found a ship going to the city of Tarshish. Jonah was trying to run away from God.

While he was on the boat, God sent a great wind which turned into a terrible hurricane as it sped across the sea. The boat that Jonah was in seemed ready to break apart.

The sailors on the boat began to pray to their gods. Then they threw all the cargo on board into the water. They were hoping that if the boat was lighter, it would sail above the giant waves and not sink.

But, instead of helping, Jonah fell asleep in his bed. The captain of the ship did not like this.

"Why are you sleeping?" he yelled. "Get up and pray to your God. Maybe your God will save us."

Then the sailors said, "Let's draw straws to see who is responsible for this storm."

They drew straws, and the short straw was picked by Jonah.

"What did you do?" They asked him. "Who are you? Where do you come from?"

"I am a Jew," Jonah told them. "God is the One I fear." Then Jonah told them how he was trying to run away from God.

The sailors became more afraid than ever. "What have you done!" they cried. "What must we do to you to get God to stop the storm?"

Jonah said, "Throw me into the sea and the storm will stop."

But the sailors didn't want to do this. Instead, they started rowing harder than before, hoping to make it to shore. But the sea became stormier than ever.

Now, the sailors prayed to God, saying, "Please don't let us die because of this man. We are innocent!" But the storm continued.

Finally, the sailors realized they had no choice. They threw Jonah into the sea. The sea immediately returned to normal.

God had a huge fish swallow Jonah, and Jonah remained in the fish's stomach for three days. Then Jonah prayed to God.

God, You threw me into the sea.

The waters whirled around me.

The seaweed wrapped around my head.

I thought I would die.

But God, You kept me alive.

*I remembered You, God, even when I thought
I might die.*

I made new promises to You, God,

And I promise to fulfill them.

God had the fish throw up Jonah onto dry land. Once again, God spoke to Jonah, saying:

"Get up and go to the great city of Ninveh and announce what I tell you."

So Jonah got up and went to Ninveh. It was such a big city that it took an average person three days to walk across it. Jonah walked into the city and shouted:

"Forty days more and Ninveh will be destroyed!"

The people of Ninveh believed Jonah. They stopped doing wicked things. They begged God for forgiveness.

Even the king took off his royal robes and put on worn, old clothes. He sent a decree across the land, saying:

"Men and cattle shall eat nothing.
Everyone is to wear old clothes.
Everyone is to call out to God,
and stop their wicked ways.
Start asking God
to forgive you now,
so that we don't all perish!"

God saw that they were serious about wanting forgiveness. So God forgave them.

But Jonah was not happy. After all, prophets had come before to Israel, saying, "Stop being wicked!" and the people had not listened. Now, Jonah was sure, the people of Israel would get punished. After all, the people of Ninveh weren't even Jewish and they listened to God. Wouldn't God be angry that the Jewish people refused to listen to the prophets? Jonah was embarrassed for his people.

"God, I would rather die," Jonah said, "than continue to live."

"Why does it bother you so much that I saved these people?" God asked Jonah.

Jonah went out of the city and built himself a little sukkah and sat under it. He wanted to see if the city would really be saved.

The shade of the sukkah was not enough to shield Jonah from the hot sun. So, God made a special plant grow above Jonah to help shade him from the sun.

Jonah was very happy.

Then God made a worm that destroyed the plant.

The heat beat down on Jonah. He was terribly hot and thirsty. And he was angry that the plant was dead.

"I would rather die, than live like this!" Jonah told God.